Thanksgiving

BY
Jane Duden

CRESTWOOD HOUSE
New York

Library of Congress Cataloging-in-Publication Data
Duden, Jane.
  Thanksgiving

  p.   cm.—(Holidays)
  Includes bibliographical references.
  Summary: Discusses the history and customs of Thanksgiving and how the holiday is celebrated
around the world.
  1. Thanksgiving Day—Juvenile literature. [1. Thanksgiving Day.] I. Title. II. Series: Holidays
(New York, N.Y.)
GT4975.D83   1990   394.2'683—dc20   89-25397   CIP
ISBN 0-89686-503-7   AC

Photo Credits
Cover: Photo Researchers: (George Haling)
AP—Wide World: 4, 25
Culver Pictures, Inc.: 7, 8, 9, 11, 17, 19, 31, 37, 38, 42
Journalism Services: 12, 20, 28, 41; (Chris Marona) 26
Berg & Associates: (Nadine Orabona) 22; (Cy Furlan) 40
DRK Photo: (Don & Pat Valenti) 23; (Stephen Krasemann) 45

Macmillan Publishing Company
866 Third Avenue
New York, NY 10022
Collier Macmillan Canada, Inc.

CRESTWOOD HOUSE

Printed in the United States

First Edition

10 9 8 7 6 5 4 3 2 1

Introduction

Crowds cheered, flags waved, and brass bands played marches. The *Mayflower* pulled into Plymouth Bay, Massachusetts. It was a great day for Americans. Seventeen-year-old Joseph Meany, Jr., of Waltham, Massachusetts was on deck. Joseph had been aboard the *Mayflower* since it left Plymouth, England, weeks before.

This probably does not sound like the *Mayflower* story you learned in school. Still, it is true. This *Mayflower* landing took place in 1957. The ship was a model of the one that brought the Pilgrims to America. On Thanksgiving Day 1957, the *Mayflower II* was given to the people of the United States by England. Today, it is anchored in Plymouth Bay. More than half a million visitors see it each year.

Joseph Meany, Jr., had been chosen to make the trip after winning the Junior Citizenship Award of the Boys' Club of America. Joseph and the crew of 33 crossed the ocean in the *Mayflower II*. The ship was just 90 feet long and 25 feet wide. The crew enjoyed a few extras unknown to the Pilgrims. *Mayflower II* had a two-way radio and a generator to make electricity. The crew also knew they would be welcomed with food, fanfare, families, and friends.

It wasn't so for the Pilgrims who sailed from England in 1620. They had no idea what awaited them. And they had no idea that the Thanksgiving celebration they held in 1621 would become the oldest, most American holiday. Hundreds of years later, Americans still celebrate Thanksgiving to honor the Pilgrims who came on the *Mayflower*.

For many across the country who watch the procession on television, Thanksgiving begins with the Macy's Parade in New York City.

America's Oldest Holiday

The *Mayflower* left England on October 16, 1620, carrying 102 English colonists. The passengers included 40 Pilgrims. The others were colonists hired by English merchants to start a new colony in America – the New World discovered by explorer Christopher Columbus in 1492. Today we usually refer to the whole group of *Mayflower* passengers as the Pilgrims.

In Search of Religious Freedom

In the 1600s, the Pilgrims in England had been part of a group of Protestants called Puritans. The Puritans wanted to purify the Church of England and change some of its rules. Some Puritans, known as Separatists, rebelled against the Church of England. They fled to Leiden, Holland. They did not enjoy Dutch city life, however. They longed for the farming life they were used to. They did not want their children learning Dutch customs and languages. They wanted their children to remember their own traditions. Explorers and traders had described the New World as a land of freedom and plenty. They hoped America would be a place where they could worship freely and build new lives. After 12 years in Leiden, they returned to England. There they prepared for the voyage across the Atlantic Ocean to America and religious freedom.

A painting of Pilgrims praying before they sailed to the
New World

The ship that brought the first English settlers to Massachusetts in 1620 was the Mayflower. The boat carried 102 people, and the trip took 66 days.

Hardships and Helpers

The Pilgrims spent 66 days at sea. On December 21, 1620, the *Mayflower* landed on the coast of what is now Massachusetts. During the voyage, the Pilgrims' supplies had been nearly used up. They could not plant crops when they landed because it was winter. The Pilgrims faced hunger and disease. They also feared the Native Americans in this strange, new land. Of the 102 Mayflower passengers, 47 did not live through the winter. It was only with the help of the Wampanoag, a friendly Native American tribe, that the Pilgrims at the Plymouth settlement survived.

This monument in Plymouth, Massachusetts, is engraved with the names of the 47 settlers who died that first winter in New England. Only 55 of the Mayflower's passengers survived.

But the best friend the Pilgrims had was a Patuxet Native American named Squanto. He was one of the first Native Americans to make peace with the settlers. Squanto had learned to speak English after he had been captured and taken to England as a slave. When Squanto returned to America, he found no Patuxets. They had all died of smallpox. After Squanto went to visit the Pilgrims in 1621, he never left them again. Squanto brought them Indian corn and taught them how to hunt game and net fish.

Giving Thanks for a Bountiful Harvest

The fall of 1621 brought a good harvest to Plymouth Colony. The Pilgrims' fears were calmed. They would survive the coming winter without starving. The grateful Pilgrims were ready to celebrate. They had chosen William Bradford to serve as the governor of their colony. With the good harvest of 1621, Governor Bradford proclaimed a three-day feast. He invited the Native Americans to join them. The first Thanksgiving took place sometime between September 21 and November 9, 1621. For three days, the four surviving adult women prepared food. Imagine their surprise when over 90 Native Americans showed up to join the 55 Pilgrims! The Native Americans brought five deer to be made into stew. The women roasted turkey, geese, and ducks. They cooked lobsters, eels, clams, oysters, and fish. There were sweet potatoes, cranberries, dried fruit, and Indian pudding, made of corn boiled with molasses. There even may have been popcorn balls, which had been invented by the Native Americans in that area.

The Wampanoag shared their food with the Mayflower's passengers.
They also taught the settlers how to fish and farm in the New World.

SUNDAY MAGAZINE
Of the SUNDAY RECORD-HERALD

COPYRIGHT, 1906, BY ASSOCIATED SUNDAY MAGAZINES INCORPORATED

CHICAGO, ILL. NOVEMBER 25, 1906

HERBERT PAUS

PART 3   20 PAGES

The joyous celebration included wrestling, racing, singing, and games. The Pilgrim children taught their favorite games to the Native Americans. There was unity, friendship, and plenty of food.

Other Thanksgivings

Some people say the settlers of Virginia's Jamestown had the first Thanksgiving in the early 1600s. They may have had a holiday based on the Harvest Home festivals of England. Others say the first Thanksgiving was held on December 4, 1619. That was the day 39 English settlers arrived at Berkeley Hundred, near today's Charles City, Virginia. The group vowed that their arrival day would be observed yearly as a day of thanksgiving to God. There was no feasting. They were not able to keep their vow, however. A few years later they were all killed in battle with Native Americans.

Maine, too, claims the first Thanksgiving. Settlers led by Captain George Popham met with Native Americans in 1607 to pray and share a harvest feast. The colony failed, so this was a one-and-only Thanksgiving, too.

What about the claims of Texas and Florida for the first Thanksgiving? On May 23, 1541, Francisco Vasquez de Coronado, a Spanish explorer, held a service of thanksgiving. Coronado and his men were searching for gold in what is now the Texas Panhandle. Instead of gold, the weary group found fresh water, food, and pasture for their horses. They stopped to give thanks. In Florida, a small French settlement of worshipers sang and prayed in thanks on June 30, 1564. Their colony near present-day Jacksonville was wiped out in 1565 by a Spanish raiding party.

Praying Pilgrims remind people that the holiday originally was created to thank God for food, shelter, and life itself.

Plymouth was different from all of these because it became a permanent settlement. The Pilgrims' thanksgiving celebration was repeated. But scholars tell us it is not accurate to say Thanksgiving began in one place and one year. Rather, our oldest American holiday gradually grew in Puritan New England. It spread and changed as the nation grew.

Harvest Festivals: An Ancient Custom

Long before the Pilgrims settled in America, people in other lands had days or seasons of thanksgiving. Many cultures have celebrated their harvests. Farmers created rituals to please spirits. They believed the spirits caused the crops to grow or fail. A good harvest was important. It meant survival.

The ancient Greeks held nine-day feasts. They honored Demeter, goddess of harvests. The Romans honored Ceres, goddess of grain, in their festival called Cerealia. The Egyptians honored Min, the god of plants.

In the Middle Ages between ancient and modern times (about A.D. 500 to A.D. 1450), a harvest festival called Martinmass was celebrated in Europe. In England, Harvest Home festivals were a yearly event. Each family celebrated after the last crop was brought in. Soon, the farmers in an area joined together for one big celebration. When the last of the grain was cut, it was loaded onto a cart. The people decorated it with green branches, flowers, and ribbons. They chose a Lord and Lady of the Harvest to ride on the cart. In some parts of England, food from the harvest was given to the needy as a gesture of sharing.

The Native Americans also had harvest festivals. Long before the Pilgrims arrived, the Iroquois celebrated an autumn festival. They called it the Green Corn Dance. They feasted on corn to begin the new year. Even tribes that did not farm but lived by gathering wild fruit or plants held harvest festivals. They celebrated when their favorite foods were in season.

Today, most people in the United States do not have to rely on food they grow themselves. It can be hard to remember that a good harvest used to mean the difference between life and death.

Three Centuries of Change

A Yankee Beginning

For years, Thanksgiving was the main holiday of the year in New England. It was a solemn day of prayer. A meal was followed by more worship and prayer. The Puritans thought holidays such as Christmas and Easter had too many pagan (non-Christian) customs mixed in. They remembered them with church services, but refused to make them merry. Still, the Puritans wanted a holiday.

The custom of setting aside special days for thanks spread among the colonies. But each colony celebrated for different reasons and on different days. Some were purely religious days, separate from any celebration of the harvest. Days for giving thanks were declared by churches and later by governors of the various states. By the start of the 1700s, the governors of Connecticut, Massachusetts, and New

Hampshire had proclaimed that a thanksgiving day be celebrated every autumn. The day should include prayer and feasting. Though other colonies often had special days of thanks, no one west or south of New England celebrated Thanksgiving. It was a holiday born and created in that part of the country.

Thanksgiving Throughout the Land

The years passed. The colonists fought the American Revolution for independence from England. In 1777, the Continental Congress declared the first official Thanksgiving Day for all 13 states. It was a day of thanks for victory in war. Congress continued the custom for the next seven years.

Thanksgiving in 1784 was the last nationwide Thanksgiving until 1789. That year, America's first president, George Washington, once again proclaimed a day for thanksgiving.

People in other parts of the country did not want to celebrate a New England holiday. They believed in the idea of thanksgiving. But they wanted to celebrate it in their own ways. By 1817, New York State had an official Thanksgiving Day. By the late 1840s, other states followed New York's example. Settlers moving westward wanted to keep their old holidays in the new territories. One after another, the western states each proclaimed a Thanksgiving Day. By then, Americans throughout the land accepted the idea that the Pilgrims had founded this nation at Plymouth Rock. They felt Thanksgiving should be celebrated by every state in the Union. The story of Pilgrims and Thanksgiving seemed good choices for a national history and a nationwide holiday.

A plump turkey is brought to a Thanksgiving table in early New England. The head of the household looks eager to carve.

An All-American Holiday

As New England settlers moved west, yearly trips back east for Thanksgiving became common. The settlers went back for family gatherings, church services, turkey dinners, and village socials. By then the Puritan religion had faded. The country had grown in every direction. New generations were not as familiar with the serious New England Thanksgiving. The quiet old holiday began picking up lively new customs.

New Yorkers added high-spirited costume masquerades and elegant balls. In the early 1900s, the children of New York had Thanksgiving customs all their own. They dressed in costumes, put makeup on their faces, and scurried through the streets begging for coins. "Anything for Thanksgiving" was their greeting to the grown-ups they hoped would give them pennies. The custom ended about 1940, but others came along.

Some Americans had public military parades on Thanksgiving. In colder northern states, the day became a time for ice-skating or sleigh rides. Evening concerts were held in some cities. More and more people celebrated by playing sports. Thanksgiving Day was a time for horse racing, dog racing, or the all-American favorites of football and baseball. By the 1890s, the Thanksgiving football game was beginning to outshine the family holiday dinner.

Thanksgiving in the Wild West had its own customs. There were holiday dinners in saloons. Neighbors were invited for dinners and dances or balls. Hunting wild game for the table was a western Thanksgiving custom. Elk, deer, and buffalo joined the turkey on the menu. There was more adventure in the West, but the basic themes of Thanksgiving were the same. People wanted to feast, entertain family and friends, and enjoy the dishes and customs of their childhoods.

The kitchen is a busy scene before this Thanksgiving feast in the mid-1880s. The girls pluck fresh birds, while the boy at the right churns butter.

Two mischievous children at a Thanksgiving table in an illustration drawn in 1904.

The 20th Century

The pull between a quiet Thanksgiving and the wish for a happy and lively holiday continued into the 20th century.

In the early 1900s, more and more immigrants came to live in the United States. Schools made sure all children learned the story of the first Thanksgiving. There were plays and pageants, poems and songs. The children were eager to be real Americans. They taught their families about Thanksgiving.

After World War II, Americans developed new ways of thinking and living. Rural life gave way to life in cities and suburbs. Wartime had brought many jobs. People had more money to spend. Advertisers and merchants began to use the holiday as a start to the Christmas shopping season. Thanksgiving kept on changing.

Thanksgiving Today

Gathering Together

The day before Thanksgiving is the year's busiest travel day. For many, Thanksgiving weekend is the longest, least interrupted weekend of the year. It is an ideal time for families and friends to gather together.

Thanksgiving dinner is a main event of the day. The menu does not change much. In most places, people know what to expect. In 1914, the famous cookbook author Fanny Farmer offered a Thanksgiving menu that is still a guide. She suggested roast stuffed turkey,

The native American turkey has become a tradition of Thanksgiving dinner.

giblet gravy, cranberries, mashed potatoes, creamed onions, and oyster and chicken pie. Dessert was plum pudding and mincemeat or pumpkin pie. But each region and each family may add its special favorites. These are all foods native to America, fitting for our national feast. Thanksgiving is still the time described in Lydia Maria Child's poem from the 1800s, "Over the River and Through the Woods." It is still the time to cheer, "Hurrah for the fun! Is the pudding done? Hurrah for the pumpkin pie!"

Sports and Games

In the 1860s, people played local baseball games on Thanksgiving afternoons. By the 1880s, football games had become the highlight of Thanksgiving. Football had become the national Thanksgiving Day sport. Each year since 1934, the Detroit Lions have played a Thanksgiving Day football game. College and professional football games have become American Thanksgiving traditions. Some families make their own games and sports rather than watch them on TV. Instead of falling asleep in a chair after their turkey dinners, they head for the ice-skating pond or dig out a favorite board game like Monopoly.

Football games are another Thanksgiving Day staple. Here Chicago trounces Washington's team.

Parades and Sales

Some cities have big Thanksgiving Day parades that are broadcast live on television. In 1921, Gimbel's Department Store in Philadelphia had the first Thanksgiving Day Parade to start the Christmas buying season.

Macy's Department Store in New York hosts an annual Thanksgiving Day Parade that has become the most well-known parade in American history. Since 1924, Macy's and other stores have been reminding people of the holiday season and marking the official arrival of Santa Claus. People watch turkeys, Pilgrims, models of the *Mayflower*, and scenes of the first Thanksgiving. Fabulous floats parade down Broadway. Bands march, movie stars wave, and giant balloons glide down the parade route. Santa Claus waves from a float. Children are dazzled by scenes of Santa's workshop and new toys.

The parades tell shoppers that Thanksgiving is here and Christmas is coming. The day after Thanksgiving is the busiest shopping day of the year. Many people enjoy the extra day off by Christmas shopping. Newspapers are filled with ads for special holiday sales. Stores are jammed with shoppers. And retailers look forward to the holiday buying season that often brings half the year's total profits. Today, Thanksgiving is more than the oldest American holiday. It has become the official opening of the Christmas season.

Music

In the first celebrations of the Thanksgiving holiday, many people sang Psalms from the Bible. But as the holiday began to stress the

Spiderman slinks down Broadway during the Macy's Thanksgiving Day Parade. He is a 78-foot-long balloon.

- The horn of plenty once represented the abundant harvests for which farmers hoped. Now it stands for the abundant meal many lucky Americans enjoy.

freedom of America and the togetherness of family, a new choice of songs came along. One song popular in the 1800s and still heard today is "Over the River and Through the Woods." Worshipers at Thanksgiving Day services still sing standards like "Come, Ye Thankful People, Come" and "Prayer of Thanksgiving." On Thanksgiving Day, radio stations also begin to play Christmas carols.

Holiday Signs and Symbols

Some things never seem to change. Today's Thanksgiving tables and school bulletin boards display familiar holiday symbols. Turkeys and Pilgrims, Indian corn, and cornucopias are symbols of this holiday.
· The cornucopia is also called a horn of plenty. It is a cone-shaped horn often used as a table centerpiece. It is filled with fruit, nuts, vegetables, and sometimes flowers. The horn of plenty stands for the harvests of Thanksgiving.

Indian corn is another symbol seen in the harvest season and at Thanksgiving. Many people gather three or more ears of Indian corn and tie them together with a ribbon. They hang the corn on the door or over the fireplace. Indian corn reminds people of how the Native Americans showed the Pilgrims how to plant and grow corn. Even though Indian corn is not a traditional Thanksgiving food, it is still an important symbol of the holiday.

Nothing says Thanksgiving like a plump golden turkey. The turkey is a common decoration on Thanksgiving greeting cards,

The Thanksgiving cover of a 1912 magazine featured a bountiful harvest.

napkins, paper plates, and tablecloths. Even though the turkey is native to America, the Pilgrims and other early settlers were already familiar with raising and eating turkey. Christopher Columbus had acquired a taste for turkey and brought the birds back to Europe. Wild turkeys, native to America, were served at the first Thanksgiving. Some birds were gifts of the Indian guests, and others had been hunted by the Pilgrims.

Early Americans often raised their own Thanksgiving turkeys. When they moved from farms to villages or big towns, they began to buy their turkeys. In some families, turkey was eaten only on special occasions. Thanksgiving dinner was such an occasion.

Remembering Others

Another tradition of Thanksgiving is remembering others. In times past, people prepared Thanksgiving baskets. They were filled with corn, chicken, potatoes, and pumpkins. Children took these baskets to the homes of the needy. Today, help for the less fortunate often comes through churches and community groups. Many people contribute to food drives. Some have special food shelves set up to help the poor. Some Americans today eat nothing on Thanksgiving. They want to remind themselves of the hunger felt by poor people. These people do not spend money on a Thanksgiving meal. They donate money to help relieve hunger around the world.

Thanksgiving and the Presidents

Changing Days and Dates

When the Constitution was adopted in 1789, President George Washington named November 26 as a day of thanksgiving. It honored the founding of a government that offered liberty, freedom, and justice for all. Six years passed before he proclaimed another Thanksgiving Day in 1795.

Thomas Jefferson, our third president, did not issue any Thanksgiving proclamation. He believed that matters of church and government should be kept separate.

Over the next decades, only Presidents John Adams and James Madison proclaimed Thanksgiving celebrations. Three years after the end of the War of 1812, President Madison proclaimed a day of Thanksgiving for peace. The other presidents left the decision about a Thanksgiving Day to the governor of each state. People had differences of opinion about the right of a government to declare a national religious holiday.

Abraham Lincoln's Proclamation

There was a growing movement to set one Thanksgiving Day that would be honored by the whole nation. In 1846, Mrs. Sarah Josepha Hale began her one-woman campaign for a single national Thanksgiving Day. Mrs. Hale was the founder and editor of *Godey's Lady's Book*, a popular magazine. She devoted each November issue of her magazine to the idea of one Thanksgiving. For nearly 40 years, she wrote articles urging the country to unify the holiday. She published features on how to celebrate it properly.

In the early 1860s, the Civil War divided America. Mrs. Hale wrote letters to the governors of every state and territory. She asked that a national Thanksgiving Day be proclaimed. She also wrote to the president. At last she found a president who would listen.

When Thomas Jefferson became president, he said that the government could not make free people celebrate Thanksgiving because it was essentially a religious holiday.

In 1863, President Lincoln announced not one, but two days of thanksgiving. The first was in August. It celebrated the victory of the Union Army at Vicksburg. Lincoln hoped the victory would mean a return to peace. On October 3, a nationwide Thanksgiving Day was proclaimed. It was to fall on the last Thursday of November 1863. That day would not be for celebrating war victories. It instead would be for giving thanks for all the blessings of Americans. This was the Thanksgiving Day that finally made Thanksgiving a national, yearly holiday. It also made Thanksgiving the last Thursday of November each year.

President Roosevelt Changes Thanksgiving

For the next 75 years, Thanksgiving was celebrated on the last Thursday of November. Then in 1939 President Franklin D. Roosevelt set Thanksgiving one week earlier.

In the late 1930s, the United States was coming out of the Great Depression. The Depression had brought years of hunger and poverty. Store owners were worried because Thanksgiving fell on November 30 in 1939. The late Thanksgiving left only 20 shopping days until Christmas. That was not enough time for the big sales that retailers needed. The retailers asked President Roosevelt to move Thanksgiving to the third Thursday. Shoppers would have an extra week for Christmas shopping.

President Roosevelt was happy to help retailers. He jolted the nation by changing the date of Thanksgiving to November 23. He did not expect the uproar that followed. Dozens of high schools and colleges played the last football games of the season on Thanksgiving Day or that weekend. Football coaches raised a fuss because they had already scheduled the ''big game'' for what they thought would be a holiday. Some people argued that there was no reason good enough for changing the date of a holiday. They felt Christmas buying should have nothing to do with Thanksgiving.

President Roosevelt's proclamation was official only in the District of Columbia. State governors could set Thanksgiving as they wished. Some began to call November 23 the Democratic Thanksgiving. November 30 was called the Republican Thanksgiving. On which day would banks be closed? On which day would workers have a day off? On which day would restaurants, railroads, and airlines serve turkey dinners? On which day would schools close? When the dust settled, 23 states celebrated on November 23. An equal number waited until November 30. Texas and Colorado observed both!

The Fourth Thursday in November

Two more years of holiday confusion followed. But when World War II began, people were more concerned about the fighting. The change in dates had not helped Christmas sales greatly. President Roosevelt signed a bill on November 26, 1941, restoring the fourth Thursday in November as Thanksgiving. It remains the permanent date of America's holiday.

Giving Thanks Around the World

The U.S. Territories

Today Thanksgiving is proclaimed each year by the president and by the governors of each of the fifty states. Since Thanksgiving is a legal holiday throughout the nation, U.S. territories observe it as a holiday, too. That means the fourth Thursday in November is Thanksgiving in the Panama Canal Zone, Guam, Puerto Rico, and the U.S. Virgin Islands. (Territories are controlled by our federal government, but they do not have equal status with states.)

The people of the Virgin Islands, an American territory in the Caribbean, celebrate two Thanksgivings. Since the Virgin Islands are often struck by hurricanes, the islanders pray for their safety during July and the following hurricane season. Then, on October 19, if there have been no hurricanes, a Hurricane Thanksgiving Day is celebrated. The islanders give thanks and pray for safety again during the next year. The second Thanksgiving in the Virgin Islands is the national American Thanksgiving each November.

Alaska and Hawaii were U.S. territories that received statehood. Before they became territories, they had their own special thanksgiving festivals.

Ancient Hawaiians had been celebrating the world's longest thanksgiving even before the English settled in America. Their festival was known as Makahiki. Makahiki lasted from November through February. During the four months of Makahiki, work and war were forbidden. Each village brought offerings of thanks to Lono, the Hawaiian god of plenty. The people then feasted, sang, and danced the hula. There were sports and war games mixed in with the merrymaking. Hawaiians today celebrate the American Thanksgiving Day and a version of the Makahiki.

Another special Thanksgiving festival was celebrated by the Inuit of Alaska. Their harsh climate did not permit a long festival. They celebrated the springtime harvest of whales, one of their most important foods. After the whale hunt ended successfully, they enjoyed chanting, drumming, dancing, singing, and games. One of the games involved using a large piece of walrus hide as a trampoline. The hide was held taut by a circle of men. One man jumped onto it and was tossed high into the air. With each toss, he tried to keep his balance and land on his feet to be tossed again.

Thanksgiving Day in Canada

There was a time when the United States and Canada celebrated Thanksgiving on the same Thursday in November. Canada decided November was too far beyond their harvest time. In 1957, the government changed the official date to the second Monday in October. Canadians now have a three-day weekend closer to their own time of harvest.

Canadian Thanksgivings are a time for families and friends to share feasts and give thanks. Like the American Thanksgiving, the Canadian holiday has its roots in Harvest Home festivals and public days of thanksgiving. It has nothing to do with Canada's founding. Canadians do not have parades or football games as Americans do.

The first official Canadian Thanksgiving was proclaimed in 1871. It celebrated the return to health of the Prince of Wales, the eldest son of England's Queen Victoria. England ruled Canada until 1867. The ties are still strong today. It wasn't until 1879 that Thanksgiving became a national yearly holiday to celebrate the blessings of the land.

Around the World

Most countries still celebrate some form of thanksgiving for good harvests. St. Martin's Day, November 11, is celebrated in northern Europe. Since St. Martin was the patron saint of beggars, children in Holland sometimes pretend to be beggars on St. Martin's Day. They go from door to door, carrying lanterns and asking for cakes, fruit, or candy. Sweden celebrates St. Martin's Day with a feast of roast goose. In the evening, the children have a parade. They carry lanterns made from candles carried in hollowed-out vegetables. In the Swiss capital of Bern, the farmers bring their produce to sell at booths on the Monday before the last Thursday in November. The festival ends with a parade through the streets in which Swiss children carry lanterns made from hollowed-out turnips.

Since World War II, the Japanese have had a national holiday to celebrate the success of farming and other occupations. They give thanks for their blessings, and government offices close for the day.

Wartime Thanksgivings

People have celebrated Thanksgiving Day even during wartime. During World War II, American soldiers celebrated Thanksgiving all over the world.

Americans of the 1850s enjoy a Thanksgiving feast.

A drawing of the first Thanksgiving done for *Ladies Home Journal*

In 1941, soldiers based in Hawaii, Greenland, and Newfoundland ate turkey on Thanksgiving Day. But soldiers in Iceland postponed their celebration. Their shipment of turkeys and cranberries was late, so they decided to wait for it.

In 1942, American soldiers in England gave away their Thanksgiving turkeys to the wounded in British hospitals. They ate roast pork, applesauce, and plum pudding for their holiday dinner. Many English people felt sorry for the U.S. soldiers who would miss families and home on Thanksgiving. They set up parties to gather the soldiers together with English families, friends and children. They hoped it would ease the soldiers' loneliness.

Each Thanksgiving during World War II, the U.S. Army promised to serve fresh turkey and not to serve anyone canned turkey. On Thanksgiving Day in 1944, soldiers stood ankle-deep in battlefield mud to get fresh turkey, mashed potatoes, gravy, and pumpkin pie for their Thanksgiving feast. Finally, in 1945, the war was over and Americans gave thanks for a world at peace.

The Spirit of Thanksgiving

Thanksgiving has been celebrated for more than 350 years. It is one of the few American holidays that different ethnic groups celebrate in many of the same ways. It is a holiday that belongs as much to Native Americans as it does to the descendants of the Pilgrims. It is a day when all Americans pause to think of the many reasons they have to be thankful.

No matter how you spend your Thanksgiving Day, you help make it special. Just as you are thankful for friendship, family, help, and care, others in your life are thankful for you. Happy Thanksgiving!

Dinner is still the main event at Thanksgiving.

A pilgrim and his wife go hunting at night.

Thanksgiving Trivia

In 1705, the town of Colchester, Connecticut, postponed its Thanksgiving ceremony because of a delay in the arrival of molasses. They couldn't make their holiday pies and puddings without it!

Sarah Hale is remembered for more than asking President Lincoln to make Thanksgiving a national holiday. She is also the author of "Mary Had a Little Lamb."

Ben Franklin wanted the turkey to become America's national bird. The other Founding Fathers won out and chose the bald eagle instead.

Tired Pilgrims set foot onshore in Massachusetts in this illustration by Currier and Ives, famous American artists.

Plimouth Plantation re-creates the life and setting of the Pilgrims' settlement. It is three miles from the first site in Plymouth, Massachusetts.

The peace and cooperation between the Pilgrims and the Wampanoag did not last. In 1675, a full-scale war broke out between the descendants of the Pilgrims and the Native Americans. The clash lasted 11 years. It caused great destruction to both sides and shattered peaceful relations.

In 1789, the Protestant Episcopal Church announced that the first Thursday in November would be a yearly day for giving thanks. That was the same year President George Washington proclaimed the first national Thanksgiving Day.

Be thankful you are not a turkey. Each Thanksgiving approximately 45 million turkeys end up in Thanksgiving ovens.

The Pilgrims did not wear the silver buckles often pictured on their hats and shoes. Not a single buckle is mentioned in any list of belongings left by the Pilgrims. They simply were not worn at that time.

President George Bush found out about his Pilgrim roots when he visited Leiden, Holland, in July 1989. The mayor of Leiden told President Bush that two of his ancestors had lived in Leiden. They had had a child and sailed on the *Mayflower*. Bush was the first U.S. president to visit the Netherlands while in office.

During his 12 years in office, President and Mrs. Franklin D. Roosevelt spent Thanksgiving at the Warm Springs Foundation. Warm Springs was founded by President Roosevelt to help polio patients. Each year, President Roosevelt, who had had polio himself, invited one of the young polio patients to share Thanksgiving dinner with him and his wife.

How did the turkey get its name? Some sources claim the Native American name for turkey was *firkee*. Others say "turkey" came from the alarm call of the bird, "turc, turc, turc." And some say it started with Christopher Columbus. He thought the New World was connected to India and that turkeys were really peacocks. He named them *tuka*, which means peacock in the Tamil language of India. Then the merchants who sold turkeys in Spain changed the Tamil *tuka* to the Hebrew *tukki*. The English later pronounced it "turkey."

The Pennsylvania Dutch ignored the traditional November Thanksgiving until the 20th century. They were actually German, which in their language was "Deutsch." Their Pennsylvanian neighbors didn't know that, and thought the newcomers were calling themselves "Dutch." The Pennsylvania Dutch disliked the Puritans, so they scorned the "Yankee" Thanksgiving. Instead, they celebrated *Arnkarch*, or Harvest Home, in church services. They decorated their churches with cornsilk, sheaves of wheat, pumpkins, squashes, and loaves of bread. At the end of each harvest service, harvest thanks offerings were collected and given to charity. Harvest Home came during the harvest, usually between July and October.

A wild turkey in full display. This bird was the forerunner of the turkey now traditionally served at Thanksgiving dinner.

For Further Reading

Here's a harvest of Thanksgiving books for reading more about the most American of all holidays.

Anderson, Joan. *The First Thanksgiving Feast.* New York: Clarion Books, 1984.

Baldwin, Margaret. *Thanksgiving.* New York: Franklin Watts, 1983.

Barth, Edna. *Turkeys, Pilgrims, and Indian Corn.* New York: The Seabury Press, 1975.

Dalgliesh, Alice. *The Thanksgiving Story.* New York: Macmillan Publishing Company, 1954.

Penner, Lucille Recht. *The Thanksgiving Book.* New York: Hastings House, 1986.

Wyndham, Lee. *Thanksgiving.* Champaign, Illinois: Garrard Publishing Company, 1963.

Index